Prologue

Why am I writing a book like this? It's not what I usually write about. Honestly, I found that over the period of many elections during my life, there were many things I was unsure about. Interestingly many people I have spoken to feel the same way. Voting is indeed a fundamental right and an integral part of democracy as it allows citizens to express their views and choose leaders who they believe will work towards improving society. However, there are several challenges that citizens face while voting, such as educating themselves about the candidates and their policies, the complexity of the election process itself, and the prevalence of misinformation and fake news.

Despite these challenges, it is essential for citizens to educate themselves and participate in the democratic process. Educating oneself about the election process, including the different voting methods, voter registration, and voter suppression, is crucial to making informed voting decisions.

The United States Constitution did not specifically define who could or could not vote, but it established how the new country would vote. Today, several amendments and laws have been passed to expand voting rights and ensure fair and equal treatment, such as the Voting Rights Act of 1965 and the 26th Amendment, which lowered the voting age to 18. This short book hopes to demystify voting in the United States. It is not meant to be comprehensive but an overview of technical and philosophical premises to help voters find traction in what may be a dystopian environment. To ensure a healthy democracy, citizens must educate themselves, participate in the democratic process, and vote. With proper education and awareness, citizens can make informed decisions and contribute to shaping the future of our country.

Chapter 1

Understanding the Election Process

As a citizen of the United States, I understand that our democratic system relies on a complex election process. This process involves a variety of activities, including primary elections, caucuses, ballot initiatives, and referendums, each with the goal of empowering citizens to participate in shaping our political landscape.

The primary elections and caucuses mark the beginning of the election process, where citizens rally behind their preferred candidates from their respective political parties. The top-voted candidate becomes the party's official nominee. During caucuses, voters assemble to discuss and endorse their preferred candidate, fostering spirited exchanges before the final vote.

Ballot initiatives and referendums are forms of direct democracy that allow citizens to propose and vote on specific policies or laws. Ballot initiatives originate from citizens, while referendums are proposed by elected officials or the government, and both appear on the ballot for voters to decide. These instruments of democracy address various issues, primarily at the state or local level, such as taxes, healthcare, and education, and the outcome of these votes can significantly impact the policies governing a particular jurisdiction.

In the United States, there is a diverse range of voting methods available, including in-person, mail-in, and early voting. In-person voting requires voters to visit designated polling locations to cast their ballots, while mail-in voting, or absentee voting, caters to those unable to vote in person on election day, such as military personnel or travelers. Early voting provides the convenience of voting in person before election day, granting voters more flexibility in scheduling their civic duty.

Voter suppression: Not new but a growing concern

Voter suppression refers to any effort or action that is intended to hinder or prevent certain groups of people from exercising their right to vote. These efforts typically target specific demographics, such as racial or ethnic minorities, low-income individuals, and young or elderly voters. The goal of voter suppression is to reduce the number of eligible voters who participate in elections, thereby influencing the outcomes in favor of certain candidates or political parties.

Various methods of voter suppression have been employed throughout history and can take different forms depending on the context. Some common tactics include:

1. Voter ID laws: Requiring voters to present specific forms of identification that may be difficult for certain groups to obtain, such as those who lack government-issued IDs or face challenges in obtaining the necessary documentation.

2. Voter registration restrictions: Imposing strict registration requirements, such as short deadlines or complex paperwork, can make it harder for eligible individuals, particularly first-time voters, to register.

3. Voter roll purges: Removing registered voters from the electoral rolls, often through methods that disproportionately affect certain communities, such as purging based on outdated or inaccurate data.

4. Reduction of early voting opportunities: Limiting the availability of early voting days or restricting early voting locations, making it harder for individuals with limited flexibility or transportation options to vote.

5. Polling place changes and closures: Closing or relocating polling stations in certain areas, leading to longer travel distances, increased wait times, and reduced access to voting facilities.

6. Gerrymandering: Manipulating the boundaries of electoral districts to concentrate or dilute the voting power of certain groups, often based on race or political affiliation.

7. Disinformation campaigns: Fake news and the spreading of false or misleading information about the voting process, such as incorrect polling dates or locations and false information about issues or candidates, in order to confuse or discourage potential voters, may be our biggest concern in 2023 and 2024.

It is important to note that voter suppression undermines the democratic principles of equal representation and participation. Many organizations and individuals actively work to combat voter suppression and advocate for fair and accessible elections.

Understanding the election process and the available voting methods empowers us to confidently and knowledgeably exercise our right to vote, ensuring that our voice is heard in shaping the future of our nation.

Chapter 2

Mastering the art of informed decision making

Embarking on the journey to make an informed decision during an election demands that we have a thorough understanding of the candidates and the issues. In this chapter, I will discuss how you can create a dynamic checklist and scoring system designed to evaluate candidates effectively based on their personal attributes, stance on key issues, endorsements, and voting history.

As a passionate voter, if you want to cast your vote for a write-in candidate, you should adhere to the following steps to ensure your vote is accurately counted:

- Consult your state's election office for eligibility, as each state has its own rules regarding write-in candidates.
- Know the candidate's name: familiarize yourself with the correct spelling of the candidate's name to circumvent any ambiguity.
- Pen the name legibly: Ensure that your handwriting is clear and legible for an accurate vote count.

When assessing presidential hopefuls, keep in mind these six pivotal personal attributes that exemplify an exceptional leader:
1. Leadership
2. Integrity
3. Empathy
4. Intelligence
5. Resilience
6. Diplomacy

To quantify each candidate based on these attributes, you can assign a score from 1 to 10, with 10 being the highest. Tallying the scores will give you a comprehensive evaluation of their personal qualities.

You should also identify up to six personal key issues and rate each candidate again on the same scale of 1-10, with 10 being the highest, according to their alignment with your priorities, to evaluate them based on your concerns.

Also, a candidate's endorsements, voting records, and history offer a wealth of insight into their values, priorities, and past actions. Therefore, you should consider these factors when making your decision.

To derive an all-encompassing score for each candidate, you can sum the scores for personal attributes, key issues, endorsements, voting records, and history. This assessment will empower you to make an informed decision when voting.

Informed decision-making during an election hinges on your careful examination of candidates and issues, guiding you to shape the future you envision.

Here are some instructions on how to create a dynamic checklist and scoring system designed to evaluate candidates effectively based on their personal attributes, stance on key issues, endorsements, and voting history. Feel free to add categories and subcategories that align with your personal concerns.

Creating a dynamic checklist and scoring system to evaluate the 2024 presidential candidates involves several steps:

Step 1: Define Categories of Evaluation

Start by defining categories that will be used for scoring.

1. Personal Attributes: These could include a candidate's personal history, communication skills, leadership ability, integrity, and more.
2. Stance on Key Issues: This involves the candidate's position on important policy areas such as the economy, healthcare, environment, etc.
3. Endorsements: The prominence and number of endorsements a candidate receives can be indicative of their popularity and acceptance among different groups.
4. Voting History: This could include how often a candidate votes, what issues they vote on, and whether their voting history aligns with their stated policy positions.

Step 2: Assign Weightage to Each Category

To give more importance to certain categories, assign a weight to each category. This could be done based on personal preference or based on the perceived importance of that category in the election. For instance, a stance on key issues might carry more weight than endorsements.

Step 3: Define Subcategories and Metrics

Within each category, define more specific subcategories and metrics for scoring. For instance, in the category of "Personal Attributes", you might have subcategories like "Leadership Skills" and "Public Speaking Ability." Each subcategory can then be scored on a scale, say from 1 to 5, where 5 represents the highest rating.

Step 4: Gather Data

Collect data on each candidate based on the defined categories and subcategories. This might involve researching the candidate's background, policy positions, voting history, etc. Sources could include the candidate's official website, reputable news sources, and databases that track voting history and endorsements like the FiveThirtyEight[3].

Step 5: Score Each Candidate

Score each candidate based on the gathered data and the defined metrics. Multiply the scores by the assigned weights for each category to get the weighted scores.

Step 6: Summarize and Analyze Results

Add up the weighted scores for each candidate to get their total score. Compare the scores to evaluate the candidates. You may also wish to create visualizations or graphs to understand the results better.

How to Use the Checklist

1. Start by defining your categories, subcategories, and metrics.
2. Assign weights to each category.
3. Conduct research on each candidate using the defined metrics.
4. Score each candidate based on your research.
5. Multiply the scores by the weights to get weighted scores.
6. Add up the weighted scores to get the total scores.
7. Compare the total scores to evaluate the candidates.
8. Update the scores as more information becomes available (e.g. if a candidate gains a new endorsement).

Remember that the results from this system are a tool to assist in understanding the candidates and should be used alongside other sources of information and personal judgment. Ultimately, the significance of these potential contenders lies in the parties' choices for nominations. Recent midterm elections demonstrated the need for principled candidates who embody the values and aspirations of the American people.

Chapter 3

Let's Get Personal

The purpose of Chapter 3 is to show you the type of personal attributes you may want to be looking for in each candidate. Things change rapidly, so make it a point to continue your research. At the end of this book are Resources for you to use. Sometimes good attributes can be found in a past President. Use the information to help create your Candidate Checklist. But then do your own research.

Joe Biden: A Steadfast Leader Eyeing a Second Term in the White House.

Joe Biden has firmly positioned himself as an unwavering figure in American politics, gaining respect from both his supporters and critics. Over the past year, his presidency and determination to secure a second term have thrust him into the forefront of the national consciousness, making him a key player in the 2024 Presidential race. Born Joseph Robinette Biden Jr. on November 20, 1942, Biden has consistently shattered expectations and risen to many challenges.

As the 46th President of the United States (2021-present), he became the oldest person to assume the office. Before his current role, he served as Vice President under Barack Obama from 2009 to 2017, and represented Delaware in the U.S Senate for six terms, evidencing his deep political experience. Biden was propelled to worldwide prominence when he successfully ran for the presidency in 2020, promising to restore the 'soul of America' after a period of significant political divisiveness.

His thoughtful leadership has garnered widespread respect and set the stage for his ongoing political career. Since his inauguration in January 2021, Biden has tackled some of the nation's most pressing issues, such as the COVID-19 pandemic, racial justice, climate change, and economic recovery, demonstrating an unwavering commitment to public service.

After assuming the presidency, Biden wasted no time in executing his mandate.

In his first year in office, he passed significant legislation, including the American Rescue Plan, which aimed to boost the economy and provide relief to Americans affected by the pandemic. His administration also focused on enhancing healthcare access, promoting renewable energy, and championing education reform.

With the 2024 presidential race on the horizon, Biden has identified critical objectives, such as improving education, expanding healthcare, addressing climate change, and ensuring economic growth. He has also underscored his commitment to social justice reform, fortifying international alliances, and managing the national debt.

Biden's demeanor is frequently described as empathetic, persevering, and principled. Recognized for his ability to bridge partisan divides and tackle complex issues with nuance and sensitivity, he brings a wealth of experience to the political landscape, resonating with a broad range of voters.

In summary, Joe Biden is a stalwart political figure with a remarkable record and a growing list of legislative achievements. As he continues to refine his political strategy and ambitions, his impact on the 2024 presidential race is inevitable. With a resilient spirit and broad appeal, Biden is set to continue making his mark on the American political scene in the years to come.

Nikki Haley: A Trailblazing Political Star with Eyes on the White House.

Nikki Haley has rapidly ascended as a dynamic force in American politics, captivating young and old alike. Over the past year, her political triumphs and presidential ambitions have become increasingly prominent, positioning her as a frontrunner for the Republican nomination in 2024. Born Nimrata Nikki Randhawa on January 20, 1972, Haley has consistently broken barriers.

As the 116th Governor of South Carolina (2011-2017), she became the first woman and individual of Indian descent to claim the title. Prior to her governorship, she represented her state in the House of Representatives from 2005 to 2010. Haley shot to national prominence in June 2015 when she demanded the removal of the Confederate flag from the South Carolina State House grounds in the wake of the devastating Charleston church shooting.

Her resolute leadership garnered bipartisan admiration and paved the way for her future political pursuits. In November 2016, President Donald Trump appointed her as the United States Ambassador to the United Nations. From January 2017 to December 2018, Haley distinguished herself with her unwavering stance on foreign policy, tough rhetoric on North Korea, and staunch support for Israel.

After departing her UN post, Haley plunged into political advocacy.

In October 2021, she launched the "Stand for America" PAC to back conservative candidates in the 2022 midterm elections. The PAC raised millions, enabling Haley to amass a formidable network of supporters and financial contributors, including billionaire Sheldon Adelson's widow, Miriam Adelson, and the Koch network.

With the 2024 presidential race in her sights, Haley has outlined pivotal objectives, such as bolstering national security, driving economic growth, and upholding American values. She has also expressed her dedication to criminal justice reform, enhancing education, and shrinking the national debt.

Haley's persona is often characterized as resolute, magnetic, and poised. Noted for her ability to collaborate across party lines and adopt a pragmatic approach to problem-solving, she brings a unique perspective to the political landscape as a woman of color and daughter of immigrants, striking a chord with a diverse array of voters.

In summary, Nikki Haley is a soaring political star with an impressive record and an expanding list of influential financial backers. As she continues to hone her political platform and ambitions, her impact on the 2024 presidential race is undeniable. With a potent persona and broad demographic appeal, Haley is set to become a powerful contender in the years to come.

Donald Trump: The Unconventional President - A Brief Overview

Donald Trump, the 45th President of the United States, led the nation from January 20, 2017, to January 20, 2021. A political outsider and billionaire businessman, Trump's journey to the White House was marked by controversy and unprecedented events.

In the months leading up to his election, Trump announced his candidacy on June 16, 2015, promising to "Make America Great Again." Trump's campaign centered on issues such as immigration, trade, and national security. His promise to build a wall along the U.S.-Mexico border and ban travelers from predominantly Muslim countries captured the public's attention.

Trump's persona as a no-nonsense, unfiltered, and unapologetic leader resonated with many Americans. On November 8, 2016, he secured an electoral victory against Democratic nominee Hillary Clinton, despite losing the popular vote.

During his office, Trump focused on deregulation, tax cuts, and appointing conservative judges. One of his most significant accomplishments was the Tax Cuts and Jobs Act, signed into law on December 22, 2017. The legislation reduced the corporate tax rate from 35% to 21%, stimulating economic growth and job creation.

Additionally, Trump's administration oversaw the appointment of three Supreme Court justices: Neil Gorsuch, Brett Kavanaugh, and Amy Coney Barrett, solidifying a conservative majority in the court.

Trump's tenure was also marked by his confrontational style and combative use of social media. His Twitter account became a primary communication tool, often overshadowing traditional media channels. Throughout his presidency, Trump frequently criticized and clashed with the press, dismissing unfavorable stories as "fake news."

On the international stage, Trump's approach was characterized by his "America First" policy. He renegotiated trade deals, including the North American Free Trade Agreement (NAFTA), which was replaced by the United States-Mexico-Canada Agreement (USMCA) on July 1, 2020. Trump also engaged in high-stakes diplomacy with North Korean leader Kim Jong-un, holding unprecedented summits in 2018 and 2019.

However, Trump's presidency was not without controversy. His administration faced criticism for its handling of the COVID-19 pandemic, which began in early 2020. The impeachment trials in December 2019 and January 2021, both of which resulted in acquittal, further polarized the nation.

Trump's presidency concluded with the contentious 2020 election, which he and many supporters claimed was fraudulent. Following the storming of the U.S. Capitol on January 6, 2021, Trump was banned from several social media platforms. Joe Biden was inaugurated as the 46th President on January 20, 2021.

Donald Trump's time in office was marked by his distinctive personality, policy accomplishments, and the controversies that surrounded him. As a political outsider, his presidency will be remembered as a unique chapter in American history.

Ron DeSantis: A Conservative Powerhouse Eyeing the White House

Ron DeSantis has rapidly become a force to reckon with in American politics, garnering attention from diverse sectors of society. Over the recent years, his political achievements and presidential ambitions have made him a major player in the Republican party, potentially eyeing a nomination for 2024. Born Ronald Dion DeSantis on September 14, 1978, he has been a figure of robust conservatism.

Serving as the 46th Governor of Florida since 2019, DeSantis has carved a strong conservative track record. Before his governorship, he represented Florida's 6th district in the U.S House of Representatives from 2013 to 2018. DeSantis gained national attention with his firm stance on immigration and tough policies on COVID-19 measures, earning both praise and criticism.

His no-nonsense leadership has gathered strong support from the Republican base and paved the path for his future political pursuits. Since becoming Governor, DeSantis has been at the forefront of several high-profile national issues, from environmental protection to education reforms, drawing both acclaim and controversy with his decisions.

After stepping into the governorship, DeSantis has actively engaged in nationwide politics.

In 2020, he was instrumental in delivering Florida for the Republicans in the Presidential Elections, demonstrating his influence within the party. His ability to rally support and manage a diverse and politically challenging state like Florida has built up a formidable network of supporters and political allies.

With the 2024 presidential race on the horizon, DeSantis has set key objectives that align with his strong conservative principles. These include implementing stringent immigration policies, promoting economic growth, and upholding traditional American values. He also champions deregulation and tax cuts, arguing that these foster a conducive environment for businesses and economic prosperity.

DeSantis's persona is often seen as assertive, steadfast, and unyielding. Known for his adherence to conservative principles and his ability to stand firm on contentious issues, he has appealed to a broad spectrum of right-leaning voters.

In conclusion, Ron DeSantis is a rising political figure with a solid record and an ever-expanding influence within the Republican party. As he continues to refine his political platform and aspirations, his potential impact on the 2024 presidential race is substantial. With a formidable persona and an appeal that resonates with many conservatives, DeSantis is set to become a serious contender in the coming years.

Vivek Ramaswamy: The Trailblazing Entrepreneur Eyeing the Oval Office

Vivek Ramaswamy, a name that has dominated business headlines recently, is now vying for the highest political office in the United States. The 37-year-old biotech entrepreneur has announced his candidacy for the 2024 presidential election, having made his intentions clear in an interview with Fox News on April 18, 2022. In the span of a year, Ramaswamy has built a formidable political profile that demands our attention. Let's explore his accomplishments, future goals, persona, and the financial backers fueling his presidential aspirations.

Ramaswamy's rise to prominence began in the biotechnology industry, where he founded Roivant Sciences in 2014. Under his leadership, the company developed innovative approaches to drug development, leading to the successful launch of several new therapies. In 2021, Ramaswamy stepped down as CEO to focus on public service and, later, his presidential bid. He has since published a bestselling book, "Woke, Inc.," in which he critiques the intersection of woke culture and corporate America.

The candidate's policy priorities are centered on a pro-business, pro-innovation platform. Ramaswamy has pledged to prioritize American manufacturing, invest in cutting-edge technology, and reduce bureaucratic red tape to spur economic growth. He has also expressed commitment to free speech and intellectual diversity, pushing back against what he perceives as the stifling influence of woke culture in American institutions.

Ramaswamy's trailblazing entrepreneur persona has garnered significant media attention and public support. He is known for his charismatic public speaking, sharp wit, and candid demeanor, which have resonated with voters across party lines. His ability to merge business acumen with policy ideas has made him a formidable contender in the political arena.

Financially, Ramaswamy's campaign has attracted several high-profile backers. Among them are tech titan Peter Thiel and venture capitalist Marc Andreessen, both of whom have been vocal supporters of Ramaswamy's pro-business, pro-innovation stance. In addition, numerous business leaders and executives from the biotech and pharmaceutical sectors have contributed to his campaign, impressed by his track record in the industry.

Vivek Ramaswamy's entry into the 2024 presidential race has made waves in American politics. His background as a successful entrepreneur, clear policy priorities, and charismatic persona have made him a candidate to watch in the upcoming election. Seeing how Ramaswamy's innovative ideas and dynamic leadership style resonate with the American electorate will be fascinating as the campaign unfolds.

Mike Pence: An Established Political Icon with a Presidential Ambition

Michael Richard Pence has cemented himself as an unwavering stalwart in the American political arena. Over recent years, his political milestones and aspirations towards the Oval Office have increasingly come to the fore, positioning him as a key contender for the Republican nomination in 2024. Born on June 7, 1959, Pence's political journey has been marked by steady progress and consistent dedication.

As the 50th Governor of Indiana (2013-2017), Pence demonstrated his commitment to conservative principles and fiscal responsibility. Before his governorship, he served his state in the House of Representatives from 2001 to 2013, earning respect for his leadership and commitment to traditional values. Pence's political prominence grew exponentially when he became the Vice President under Donald Trump's administration in 2016.

His tenure as Vice President was marked by his steady demeanor, loyalty to the Trump administration, and commitment to conservative values. Pence notably presided over the Senate during some of the most contentious moments of Trump's presidency, including the impeachment trials and the confirmation of Supreme Court justices.

Following his tenure as Vice President, Pence has continued his involvement in conservative politics and advocacy. In 2021, he launched the "Advancing American Freedom" advocacy group aimed at promoting the Trump-Pence administration's achievements and conservative values. The group has attracted a host of wealthy donors and conservative figures, signaling a robust network of supporters as he eyes the 2024 presidential race.

With the upcoming presidential election in view, Pence has highlighted key priorities such as defending conservative values, stimulating economic growth, and ensuring national security. His commitment to religious freedom, constitutional principles, and law and order continue to define his political persona.

Pence's political style is often marked as steadfast, poised, and deeply conservative. Known for his ability to navigate complex political waters with a calm and composed demeanor, he brings a distinctive perspective to the political landscape as a conservative Christian. His traditional values resonate strongly with a certain segment of the voting populace.

In summary, Mike Pence is an established political figure with a proven record and an expanding network of influential backers. As he continues to refine his political platform and aspirations, his influence on the 2024 presidential race becomes increasingly evident. With a staunchly conservative stance and widespread support within certain demographics, Pence is poised to be a significant player in the coming years.

In conclusion: Voting is a fundamental right and responsibility of citizens in a democracy. However, the election process can be complex and overwhelming, with multiple steps and vast information to consider. This book is attempting to provide a guide to navigating the election process, from understanding primary elections and caucuses to researching candidates and issues and casting your vote.

We have explored the different voting methods available, including in-person, mail-in, and early voting, and provided a checklist for writing in candidates' names. Additionally, we have provided a personal attribute scoring system, a key issue evaluation system, and space to write in each candidate's endorsements, voting records, and voting history to help voters make informed decisions when evaluating candidates.

Participating in the election process is essential to exercise your democratic rights and shaping your community and country's future. By understanding the election process and the various voting methods available and carefully researching the candidates and issues, citizens can be better equipped to make informed voting decisions.

Remember, every vote counts, and every voice matters. By participating in the democratic process, we can ensure that our values and priorities are represented in the policies and laws that govern our lives.

There are entities other than candidates that you should familiarize yourself with before an election. Chapter 5 begins with the G20.

Chapter 5

A Brief Overview of The G20

The Group of Twenty, or G20, is an international forum for governments and central bank governors from 19 countries and the European Union. Established in 1999, the G20's primary goal is to promote international financial stability and address key issues related to global economic growth, international trade, and the regulation of financial markets. The G20 brings together the world's major advanced and emerging economies, representing around 85% of global GDP, 75% of international trade, and two-thirds of the world's population.

Members:

The G20 consists of 19 individual countries and the European Union, which is collectively represented by the European Commission and the European Central Bank. The member countries are as follows:

Argentina	Japan
Australia	South Korea
Brazil	Mexico
Canada	Russia
China	Saudi Arabia
France	South Africa
Germany	Turkey
India	United Kingdom
Indonesia	United States
Italy	

In addition to the permanent members, the G20 also invites guest countries and international organizations, such as the United Nations, World Bank, and International Monetary Fund, to participate in its meetings.

History:

The G20's origin can be traced back to the financial crises of the late 1990s, particularly the Asian financial crisis in 1997 and the Russian financial crisis in 1998. These crises exposed vulnerabilities in the global financial system and highlighted the need for better cooperation among major economies to prevent similar occurrences in the future.

In response, the G7 finance ministers and central bank governors, representing the world's leading industrialized nations, convened a meeting in September 1999 to discuss the establishment of a new international forum. This forum, later known as the G20, was intended to bring together the finance ministers and central bank governors from major advanced and emerging economies to discuss and promote international financial stability.

Initially, the G20 focused on finance and economic issues, with meetings held among finance ministers and central bank governors. However, following the global financial crisis in 2008, the G20's mandate expanded to include heads of state and government, reflecting the urgent need for a more coordinated response to the crisis. The first G20 summit was held in Washington, D.C., in November 2008, where leaders agreed on a series of measures to stabilize the global financial system and prevent future crises.

Over the years, the G20 has played a critical role in coordinating global efforts to address various economic challenges, such as the Eurozone debt crisis, the promotion of sustainable development, and the fight against climate change. It has also focused on issues such as tax evasion, corruption, and the regulation of cryptocurrencies.

In conclusion, the G20 is an important international forum that brings together the world's major economies to promote international financial stability and address global economic challenges. It has evolved since its inception, expanding its mandate to include a broader range of issues and increasing the participation of heads of state and government.

The G20: Assessing Concerns about Control and Effectiveness in Global Economics and Conflicts

In the first part of this analysis, we explored the origins, members, and history of the G20. As an international forum for governments and central bank governors, the G20 has played a significant role in promoting international financial stability and addressing global economic challenges. However, concerns have been raised about the G20's control and effectiveness in global economics and conflicts. In this second part, we will discuss these concerns and their implications for the future of the organization.

There are concerns about the G20's Lack of Representation, Legitimacy, Control, and Effectiveness:
Although the G20 represents around 85% of global GDP, 75% of international trade, and two-thirds of the world's population, it has been criticized for its lack of representation and legitimacy. Many smaller and less-developed countries are

excluded from the forum, leading to concerns that their voices are not being heard on issues that directly affect them. This has led to calls for reforming the G20 to include a more diverse and representative set of countries.

Inefficient Decision-making Process:
The G20 operates on the principle of consensus, meaning that decisions are reached through extensive negotiation and compromise among member countries. While this approach promotes dialogue and cooperation, it can also lead to slow and inefficient decision-making. The lack of a formal voting mechanism makes it difficult to resolve disagreements, which can impede progress on important issues.

Limited Influence on Global Conflicts:
Although the G20 was initially established to address economic and financial issues, the organization's mandate has expanded to include various non-economic matters. However, the G20's effectiveness in resolving global conflicts and political crises has been questioned. For example, the G20 has had limited success in addressing ongoing conflicts in Syria, Ukraine, and Yemen, among others. Critics argue that the G20's focus on consensus-building may hinder its ability to take decisive action in response to urgent geopolitical crises.

Inadequate Enforcement Mechanisms:
The G20 has played a crucial role in coordinating global efforts to address economic challenges, such as implementing financial regulatory reforms and promoting sustainable development. However, the organization lacks formal enforcement mechanisms to ensure that member countries follow through on their commitments. This has led to concerns about the G20's ability to hold its members accountable and effectively implement its policy recommendations.

Conclusion:
The G20 has undoubtedly made significant strides in promoting international financial stability and addressing key global economic challenges. However, concerns about its control and effectiveness, such as lack of representation, inefficient decision-making, limited influence on global conflicts, and inadequate enforcement mechanisms, must be acknowledged and addressed. To maintain its relevance and credibility, the G20 must continue to evolve, improve its decision-making processes, and work towards more inclusive representation. By doing so, the organization can further enhance its ability to tackle pressing global challenges and promote a more stable and prosperous world.

Chapter 6

The "GOP"

What does GOP stand for? And why are Republicans elephants and Democrats donkeys?

You've probably heard of the Republican Party being referred to as the "GOP." But do you know what GOP stands for? And why are Republicans depicted as elephants and Democrats as donkeys?

We'll have to go back in history for the answers.

GOP stands for "Grand Old Party" and is often used interchangeably with the word Republican. The acronym dates back to the 1870s, about the same time the party picked up its elephant logo.

The name "Republican" dates back to 1792 and the supporters of Thomas Jefferson. The party was originally known as the Democratic-Republican Party before divisions in the 1830s led to the formation of the stand-alone Republican Party in the 1850s. The original Republican Party was made up mostly of abolitionists opposed to slavery in the South.

After the Civil War, Republicans saw their political influence grow, and in 1888, the party saw the election of Benjamin Harrison and a majority of Congress. A writer for the Chicago Tribune said the triumph represented an accomplishment by the "Grand Old Party," in referring to the Republicans.

The phrase was shortened, and GOP began showing up in stories about Republicans. There's some evidence, however, that the acronym might have started earlier, as way back as 1875, when the term "gallant old party" was used in reference to the party.

While we now use GOP and Republican almost interchangeably, it doesn't mean everyone knows what the acronym stands for. A 2011 poll showed that almost half of Republicans didn't know what the letters stood for. Some of the guesses for those who weren't sure included "Government of the People," "Grumpy Old People," and "God's Own Party."

You can blame a journalist for each party's symbols as well.

The donkey was first used by Andrew Jackson in 1828, whose employee tried to label him a "jackass." Jackson turned it around and began using the donkey on his campaign posters.

Then during the mid-term elections of 1874, Democrats were claiming President U.S. Grant would seek a third term. Thomas Nast, a cartoonist for Harper's Weekly, spoofed the idea by drawing a stubborn Democratic donkey trying to scare a docile, slow-moving elephant he said represented the Republicans.

The symbols are stuck and are used to this day. You can insert your own joke here:

Chapter 7

Dissecting Global Wealth and Influence

Who Has the Money

I've witnessed the ever-changing landscape of the world economy and its impact on society. Today, I'm more concerned than ever about the control that global economics exerts on our everyday lives and politics. Here we will delve into the factors that shape the world's power dynamics. We will attempt to identify the major players holding the world's wealth and discuss the significance of their financial power.

The global economic landscape is largely dominated by a few key players. These countries and organizations possess significant financial resources, which in turn grant them substantial influence in international politics and decision-making.

United States: As the world's largest economy, the United States remains a major player in global financial affairs[2]. Its significant military spending, advanced technology, and powerful corporations give the country the ability to shape global policies and standards.

China: Over the past few decades, China has emerged as a formidable economic power, challenging the United States' dominance. Its rapid industrialization, massive population, and expanding global investments make China a key player in international finance.

European Union: The collective economic power of the European Union (EU) member states makes the bloc a force to be reckoned with on the world stage. The EU's ability to negotiate trade deals and set regulatory standards gives its member countries significant clout in global affairs.

Multinational Corporations: Large multinational corporations, such as Apple, Google, Nvidia, and Amazon, wield significant financial influence in the global economy. The wealth and resources of these companies often surpass those of entire nations, granting them considerable power in shaping industry standards and political decisions.

Wealthy Individuals: High-net-worth individuals, including billionaires and family dynasties, hold significant financial assets that can be leveraged to influence global events. The philanthropic endeavors of these individuals often mask their more strategic investments in global enterprises and political campaigns.

In this era of globalization, the concentration of wealth and power in the hands of a select few has far-reaching consequences. As we move forward, we need to explore the geopolitical goals of these major players and evaluate their progress toward achieving their objectives.

We must examine the major players who possess the world's wealth, giving them substantial influence in international politics and decision-making. Let's delve into the geopolitical goals of these economic powerhouses, seeking to understand their strategic aims as they navigate the complex world of global economics and politics.

The United States' primary geopolitical goals include maintaining its global economic leadership, promoting democracy, and ensuring national security. The U.S. seeks to secure its position as the world's largest economy by investing in advanced technology, fostering innovation, and forging strong alliances with other nations. Additionally, the U.S. aims to strengthen its military presence worldwide to protect its national interests and deter potential adversaries.

China's geopolitical ambitions center around achieving global economic dominance, securing resources, and expanding its sphere of influence. China's rapid industrialization and massive population have fueled its pursuit of economic supremacy, leading the country to invest heavily in global infrastructure projects, such as the Belt and Road Initiative. Additionally, China aims to secure access to vital resources, such as energy and raw materials, to sustain its growing economy.

The European Union's (EU) primary geopolitical goals revolve around promoting unity among its member states, securing the bloc's economic stability, and exercising influence in global affairs. The EU seeks to maintain its collective economic power by negotiating favorable trade deals and setting regulatory standards that benefit its member countries. Additionally, the EU aims to address pressing global challenges, such as climate change and migration, through concerted diplomatic efforts.

Large multinational corporations, such as Apple, Google, Nvidia, and Amazon, have the strategic aim of increasing shareholder value while expanding their market reach and influence. These corporations often strive to shape industry standards and political decisions to create favorable business environments, secure access to resources, and protect their intellectual property.
High-net-worth individuals, including billionaires and family dynasties, often have diverse and varied geopolitical goals. Their objectives may include securing their financial assets, advancing their personal interests, and promoting their ideological beliefs. These individuals frequently leverage their wealth to influence global events, whether through philanthropy, strategic investments, or political campaign donations.

In conclusion, the major players in the global economy have unique and ambitious geopolitical goals that drive their actions on the world stage. As we move on to the third and final part of this series, we will examine the current global landscape and evaluate the progress these economic powerhouses are making toward achieving their objectives.

Evaluating Progress and Impact of Global Wealth and Influence

United States: The U.S. has continued to maintain its global economic leadership through advancements in technology and innovation[1]. However, its dominance has been increasingly challenged by the rise of China and other emerging economies. While the U.S. remains a key player in international affairs, it is facing growing competition and potential threats to its national security.

China: China has made significant progress in achieving global economic dominance, with its Belt and Road Initiative expanding its influence and securing access to vital resources[2]. However, the country has also faced criticism for its assertive approach in the South China Sea and concerns over its human rights record. These issues may hinder China's ability to fully realize its geopolitical ambitions.

European Union: The EU has made strides in promoting unity among its member states and securing the bloc's economic stability[3]. The EU's efforts to address global challenges, such as climate change and migration, have shown varying levels of success. However, the bloc continues to face internal divisions and external pressures that may threaten its long-term stability and influence.

Multinational Corporations: Companies like Apple, Google, and Amazon have continued to expand their market reach and influence, shaping industry standards and political decisions in their favor[2]. However, these corporations have also faced growing scrutiny over their business practices and the concentration of wealth and power they represent, leading to calls for increased regulation and oversight.

Wealthy Individuals: High-net-worth individuals have leveraged their wealth to influence global events through philanthropy, strategic investments, and political campaign donations[2]. While some have made meaningful contributions to society, concerns over the outsized influence of these individuals on global affairs persist.

In conclusion, the major players in the global economy have made varying degrees of progress toward achieving their geopolitical goals. However, the current global landscape is fraught with challenges and uncertainties, with the potential to reshape the balance of power and influence in the coming years. As an 18-year veteran global financial analyst and writer[1], I will continue to monitor these developments and their impact on the world economy, offering insights and analysis to help readers navigate this complex and ever-changing landscape.

Resources

Here are five of my favorite websites to conduct research on the current presidential candidates:

1. **FiveThirtyEight (URL: https://projects.fivethirtyeight.com/polls/)**
    FiveThirtyEight is a well-regarded site for its polling data, statistical analysis, and election forecasting. It's a valuable resource for understanding the current political landscape and the popular support for each candidate. FiveThirtyEight consistently aggregates and analyzes data from numerous polls, providing an unbiased, data-driven perspective of the race.

2. **RFF Candidate Tracker (URL: https://www.rff.org/publications/data-tools/candidate-tracker/)**
    The RFF Candidate Tracker is a comprehensive tool for comparing the policy positions of presidential candidates, particularly on climate and energy topics. It gathers information from a variety of sources, providing a detailed view of each candidate's stance on critical issues. The tracker is regularly updated, and it's a reliable source for understanding the policy implications of each candidate's platform.

3. **OpenSecrets (URL: https://www.opensecrets.org/)**
    OpenSecrets is an excellent resource for tracking campaign donations. Understanding where candidates get their funding can provide insight into their political alliances and the special interests that may influence their policy decisions. This tool provides transparency into the financial side of the campaigns.

4. **FactCheck.org (URL: https://www.factcheck.org/)**
    FactCheck.org is a non-partisan, non-profit website that checks the factual accuracy of political statements by politicians, including presidential candidates. With the growing issue of misinformation, this site is an essential tool for verifying the truthfulness of candidate claims.

5. **Ballotpedia (URL: https://ballotpedia.org/)**
    Ballotpedia provides comprehensive coverage of U.S. politics, including detailed profiles of every major candidate and their policy positions. It also includes information about the electoral process and helps users understand the full context of the ballot.

Remember that each of these resources provides a piece of the puzzle, and a well-rounded understanding will come from using them all. A good political analyst would look at the situation from multiple angles, cross-referencing data between these and other reliable sources.

9 798851 891731